Alexander McLeod, John N McLeod

Negro Slavery Unjustifiable

A Discourse

Alexander McLeod, John N McLeod

Negro Slavery Unjustifiable
A Discourse

ISBN/EAN: 9783744733007

Printed in Europe, USA, Canada, Australia, Japan

Cover: Foto ©ninafisch / pixelio.de

More available books at **www.hansebooks.com**

NEGRO SLAVERY

UNJUSTIFIABLE.

———•◦•———

A DISCOURSE

BY THE LATE

REV. ALEXANDER McLEOD, D.D.,

PASTOR OF THE FIRST REFORMED PRESBYTERIAN CHURCH, NEW YORK.

" Whosoever looketh unto the perfect law of liberty, and continueth therein ; he being not a forgetful hearer, but a doer of the work ; this man shall be blessed in his deed."—James i. 25.

1802.

———••◦•◦———

ELEVENTH EDITION.

WITH AN APPENDIX.

NEW YORK:

PUBLISHED BY ALEXANDER McLEOD,

57 WEST TWENTIETH STREET.

For Sale also by SINCLAIR TOUSSEY, 121 Nassau Street, and I. LANE, 264 Sixth Avenue.

1863.

Three years ago a large issue of this discourse was made. It was soon exhausted, and now there is not a copy to be found in market. Many calls are made for it from various quarters. No pecuniary emolument has come to the publisher from it. He gave it as a part of his contribution in both private and public station, to the principle and cause of emancipation. And he sends it forth again to aid that sacred cause, whose progress has been so rapid and triumphant for the past two years. Believing that Slavery has made the tyranny that has produced the rebellion and the war, that the emancipation policy is necessary to the salvation of the National life, and that the time for the exodus of the oppressed millions of the colored race among us has come, he gives the "Sermon" again to the country. The Appendix will show that the pulpit of the First Reformed Presbyterian Church, New York, still speaks for Liberty.

Entered according to Act of Congress, in the year 1863, by
ALEXANDER McLEOD,
In the Clerk's Office of the District Court of the United States for the Southern
District of New York.

PUBLISHER'S PREFACE.

The first edition of this Discourse was printed in this city just sixty-one years ago. It has been often published since, both in this country and in Europe; and as often it has received the commendation of the philosopher, and patriotic statesman, as well as the christian to whom its demonstrations are more immediately addressed. A copy of the first edition was sent to Thomas Jefferson, and was the occasion of a correspondence between him and its author, on the whole subject of the colored race in the United States, and the best means of doing it good. Another copy found its way into the hands of that celebrated philanthropist, Henry, Count Gregoire of France. He speaks of it in highly complimentary terms, and "couples its author with Mr. Jefferson, as a defender of the rights of humanity."

Dr. Alexander McLeod was well known in the city of New York for many years, as an eloquent preacher, able theologian, and clear and earnest writer on the morals of politics. As a true patriot he reproved the faults of his adopted country, while he defended her rights. Carrying out the creed of his church, he tried all things by the Bible, and proclaimed its supremacy as well over social institutions, as over personal character. There were but few, in the day when he wrote, to vindicate slavery in America as right and beneficial in itself, much less as approved in divine revelation. It was then, rather viewed, even by its apologists, as an admitted evil of which it was difficult to dispose, than a good deserving perpetuation. Now it is extensively proclaimed to be a political necessity, a moral institution, a Bible appointment. Against such deceptive error, the Discourse brings to bear its strong batteries of Scripture logic, sustained by historical fact, and economical deduction. And it shows that "the practice of buying, holding, or selling our unoffending fellow creatures as slaves is immoral," and of course dangerous to the individual, and the community in which it exists. In the notes, which are valuable, the opinions of such well known statesman and divines as Thomas Jefferson, Dr. Jedediah Morse, and Dr. Samuel Miller are presented. These deserve to be pondered now.

ADVERTISEMENT.

The Author of this Discourse had a call presented to him, in November, 1800, to take the pastoral charge of a congregation in the county of Orange, in the State of New York. He perceived among the subscribers the names of some whom he knew to be holders of slaves. He doubted the consistency of enslaving the negroes with the Christian system, and was unwilling to enter into a full ecclesiastic communion with those who continued the practice. He hesitated to accept the call, but took an early opportunity of writing to the Elders of the Church, and of intimating to the Presbytery his sentiments respecting slavery.

The Reformed Presbyterian Church has judicially condemned the practice, and warned their connections against it. This produced an additional evidence of the force of Christian principle. It triumphed over self-interest; and, in several parts of the United States have men sacrificed, on the altar of religion, the property which the civil law gave them in their fellow men. There is not a slave-holder now in the communion of the Reformed Presbyterian Church.

A sense of duty determined the author to commit this Discourse to the press. In the publication of it he has particularly in view the instruction and establishment of those inhabitants of Orange who have placed themselves under his pastoral care. Through them he addresses all into whose hands the Discourse may come.

If the Redeemer shall be pleased to bless it, and render it the means of ameliorating the bondage, or of procuring the liberty of any miserable African, the Author shall receive more than a recompense.

THE PRACTICE

or

HOLDING MEN IN PERPETUAL SLAVERY

CONDEMNED.

————•◆•————

" He that stealeth a man, and selleth him, or if he be found in his hand. he shall
surely be put to death."—Exod. xxi. 16.

God is omnipotent. His omnipotence is necessary,
and independent of every other being. He is the
source from which all power flows. Whatever physical force can be exerted by man, is derived from his
Maker. In the exercise of natural power, man is under
a law to God. He is indeed a free agent; but the
divine law circumscribes his sphere of action, and
marks out boundaries which he cannot pass with impunity. To exert his natural powers under the direction of law is right: to exercise any powers derived
from God, contrary to his declared will, is wrong.
Whatever is included in the grant God has made to
the human family, is one of the *rights of man*; and
beyond this grant, contrary to God's law, man cannot
claim a right, until he shakes off his dependency, and
elevates his own authority until it become paramount
to that which is exercised by Jehovah. Whosoever
attempts to deprive any of the human family of the
former, or put him in possession of the latter, is guilty
of treason against Heaven, unless he is expressly com-

missioned, in this particular instance, to contradict the general principles of law, by the same great authority from which the law derives its binding force. He who, without this authority, breaks over the barriers of law, and, with physical force, deprives his neighbor of liberty or property, is an enemy to God and to man; much more so he who commences an unprovoked attack on any of his fellow men, and, with lawless power, steals him from his connections, barters him for some other commodity, or forces him to labor for the benefit of another, and that other an *enemy*, who has committed, or countenanced the commission of the theft.

The divine law declares this a crime, and prescribes the punishment. *He who stealeth a man, and selleth him, or if he be found in his hand, he shall surely be put to death.*

This law was given to the Hebrews as a body politic; but it proceeds on a moral ground, and is, consequently, obligatory still on every subject of moral government.

He who acknowledges the morality of the eighth precept of the decalogue, will not require another proof of the morality of the conduct recommended in the text. If he who steals my purse, my coat, or my horse, be guilty of an immorality, he cannot be innocent who robs me of my father, my brother, my wife, or my child. Against this principle an inspired apostle directs his argument, in his Epistle to Timothy. 1 Tim. i. 9. *Knowing this, that the law is not made for a righteous man, but for the lawless and disobedient —for* MAN STEALERS—*and if there be any other thing that is contrary to sound doctrine.* Man stealing is classed with the most detestable crimes. It is considered not only reprehensible among the ancient Hebrews, but a moral evil in every age, and in every nation.

From the text, I consider myself authorised to lay before you the following proposition :

The practice of buying, holding, or selling our unoffending fellow creatures as slaves is immoral.

The text will certainly support this proposition. According to the common principles of law, the receiver of stolen goods, if he know them to be such, is esteemed guilty as well as the thief. The slave-holder never had a right to force a man into his service, or to retain him, without an equivalent. To sell him, therefore, is to tempt another to sin, and to dispose of that for money, to which he never had a right.

The proposition does not militate against slavery under every form. By no means. A man, by the abuse of his powers, to the injury of society, may forfeit liberty, and even life : he may deserve slavery in the fullest sense of the word, in order that his punishment may be a sanction to the law—may be an example to others—and may compensate, as much as possible, for the injuries done to society. By " innocent fellow creatures, " in the proposition, it is not designed to teach that any of the human race is so in relation to the divine law : it is not to be understood in a moral, but in a political sense. As the subjects of Jehovah's government, we are all guilty, and deserve to perish. We have merited eternal imprisonment from Him. But, in relation to civil society, men are deemed innocent unless they have violated its laws. These are assuredly entitled to personal freedom.

It is intended, in this Discourse, to *confirm the doctrine of the proposition—to answer objections to it— and make some improvement of it.*

8

1. *To hold any of our fellow men in perpetual slavery is sinful.*

1. This appears from the inconsistency of the practice of holding slaves with the *natural rights of man.* This is a term which has been much abused. It is proper that accurate ideas should be annexed to it, otherwise its force, in the present argument, will not be perceptible. If man were a being, owing his existence to accident, and not a creature of God, his rights would indeed be negative. If he stood in a state of independency of his Maker, and not a subject of law, his rights could be determined only by the will of society. But he is neither the *son of chance* nor the *possessor of independency.* His life and his faculties are the gift of God. From heaven he derives positive rights, defined by positive precepts.* Considering man as a free agent, by the constitution of na-

---

* The author of "Political Justice" maintains that the rights of man are all negative—that *man has no rights.* His reasoning is ingenious, and is certainly less absurd than that which would introduce blasphemy and vice among the rights of man. Both sentiments are, however, absurd, and the absurdity proceeds from the same source. Man is considered in relation to man only. The interest of truth requires this error to be detected and exposed. Before man is considered in relation to man, his relation to God must be understood. This is the primary one. It is that by which all others must be regulated. Consider man as a creature of God, and depending upon his bounty, and you see him receiving certain privileges from that Lord who has a necessary and absolute property in all things. *These are the rights of man.* They are not inherent, but derived.

Consider man as a creature, and you see him under a law to God. His possessions are completely circumscribed. Beyond this he has no right. *All the rights of man are derived from God, and agreeable to His law.*

By punctual attention to this principle, the friends of truth may consistently and successfully combat those who would rob man of his rights, or would unduly extend them. From this double battery, by maintaining a well-directed fire, they may defeat the supporters of civil and religious usurpation on the one side, and the propagators of licentiousness in politics and religion on the other.

ture he has a right to the exercise of freedom, in conformity to the precepts of that law by which the Author of nature has ordered him to regulate his actions. A delegated power he has from God, and no creature has a right to restrict him in its rightful exercise. To oppose the force of an individual, or of a society, to this, is to wage war against the Supreme Ruler; it is an attempt to reduce a moral agent to a mere machine, whose motions are to be regulated by external force; and, consequently, a denial of his right to the person enslaved, and an arrogant assumption of lawless authority by the usurper. Is it necessary to pursue this argument before an American audience? It is generally, if not universally admitted. The principle is stated and maintained in that instrument which lies at the foundation of your national existence. In defence of it you have fought—you have appealed to the Lord of Hosts; and in its support He has led on your armies to victory.

2. If an opposite principle of action were universally admitted, it would lead to absolute absurdity. A demonstration of this will confirm the proposition.

If one man have a right to the services of another, without an equivalent, right stands opposite and contrary to right. This confounds the distinction between right and wrong. It destroys morality and justice between man and man, between nation and nation. I have a right to enslave and sell you. You have an equal right to enslave and sell me. The British have a right to enslave the French, and the French the British—the Americans the Africans, and the Africans the Americans. This would be to expel right from the human family—to resolve law into force, and justice into cunning. In the struggle of contending rights, violence would be the only arbiter. The decisions of reason would be perverted, and the sense of morality extirpated from the breast.

Such absurdity will meet with few advocates to plead its cause in theory. Is it not, therefore, lamentable, that any should indulge a principle, or countenance a practice, the justification of which would necessarily lead to it? But,

3. The practice of enslaving our fellow men stands equally opposed to the general tenor of the Sacred Scriptures.

The Bible is the criterion of doctrine and conduct. It represents the European and the Asiatic, the African and the American, as different members of the same great family—the different children of the same benign and universal parent. *God has made of one blood all the nations of men to dwell on all the face of the earth, and hath determined the bounds of their habitation.* Acts xvii. 26. In relation to one another, they are equally bound to the exercise of benevolence, and are respected as naturally having no inequality of rights. Every man is bound to respect his fellow man as his neighbor, and is commanded to love him as himself.* Our reciprocal duties the divine Jesus summarily comprehends in that direction commonly called the golden rule: *Whatsoever ye would that men should do to you do ye even so to them; for this is the law and the prophets.*† This is the sum of the duties inculcated in the law of Moses, and in the writings of the inspired prophets. How opposite the spirit of these precepts and doctrines to the practice of the slave-holder! If he is consistent with himself, he will reason thus: "These slaves are not of one blood with me. They are not entitled to the love I give to my

---

* Mark xii. 31.   † Matt. vii. 12.

neighbor. The conduct which I should pursue, were I enslaved by another, I would not recommend to them. I shall feed and clothe them from the same principle that I feed and stable my cattle. They are my property as much as these; and when they do not serve my purpose agreeably to my wishes, I shall dispose of them for money to another trafficker in human flesh. I acknowledge, if any person was to enslave me, I should endeavor to embrace the first opportunity of making my escape. But if my negro offers to run away, I shall pursue and severely chastise him. He has no right to leave his master; the rule, Whatsoever ye would that men should do unto you, do ye also so to them, notwithstanding."—I need not add, brethren, that such sentiments are opposite to the principles of the Christian Religion.

4. The practice which I am opposing is a manifest violation of four precepts of the decalogue.

If this can be shown, it will be an additional confirmation of the doctrine of the proposition. Revelation informs us, that whosoever offends in one point is guilty of all. James ii. 10. And the reason is added, because the same authority is wantonly opposed in that one point which gives sanction to the whole of divine revelation. By inference, therefore, the whole decalogue is violated; but there is a direct breach of the fifth, the sixth, the eighth and the tenth commandments.

The *fifth* requires the performance of those duties which respect the several relations in which we stand to one another; and particularly enforces obedience to our natural parents. The Christian's duty to the wretched African, brought providentially under his care, is to afford him the necessaries of life—to bring him up in the nurture and admonition of the Lord—

to instruct him in the knowledge of his duty and his rights—to habituate him to honest industry—to help him to some.business for himself, and set him at liberty from his control. But the slave-holder exercises *often* a cruel, *always* an illegitimate, authority over his slave. He destroys, to a great degree, natural relationship. He sets aside the authority of the immediate parent; and, in opposition to the divine law, which commands each to honor his father and mother, the child is taught, from the cradle, that his duty consists in implicit obedience to the command of his master.

The *sixth* requires the use of all lawful means to preserve the lives of men. But ah! Slavery, how many hast thou murdered? Thou hast kindled wars among the miserable Africans. Thou hast carried the captive, who escaped death, into a still more miserable state. Thou hast torn from the bosom of the grieved mother her beloved daughter, and hast brought down the gray hairs of an aged parent, with sorrow, to the grave. Thou hast hurried them on board thy floating prisons, and hast chained them in holds, which have soon extinguished the remaining spark of life. The few who have escaped thou hast deprived of liberty, dearer itself than life.

The *eighth* forbids the unlawful hindrance of our neighbor's wealth. The whole life of the slave-holder is an infringement upon it. The labor of a man is worth more than his food and clothing; but the slave receives no more. His master robs him of the fruits of industry. He steals him from his relations. He robs him of his liberty of action. He steals him from himself. The *tenth* commandment forbids all inordinate desires after worldly property. The practice of the slave-holder is an evidence of his avarice. He employs servants without wages. He sells to a hard master, for money, the man and the woman whose severe services have already done more than make him compensation for any trouble or expense to which they had subjected him. Not only the avaricious merchant who sails to the coast of Africa with his ship fitted out with the implements of cruelty, in order to import and expose to sale our sable brethren; but the American slave-holder also, is convicted of a breach of the tenth precept of the moral law.

5. The system against which I contend is also inimical to that benevolent spirit which is produced and cherished by the gospel of free grace.

In the system of grace all men are represented as proceeding from one pair—as fallen from a state of integrity and happiness, into a situation that is sinful and miserable. God is revealed as beholding man in this condition with an eye of benevolence—having pity for the distressed, mercy for the miserable, and grace for the unworthy. Jesus, God in our nature, appointed as the Saviour of sinners, and without respect of persons, gathers from the North and from the South, from the East and from the West, out of every kindred, tongue, and people, and nation, an innumerable multitude, to be introduced, through His divine mediation, into a state of unspotted purity and unspeakable happiness.

The influence which the grace of the gospel has upon the heart, is to cultivate, increase, and perfect every benevolent affection, and suppress all malevolence, extirpating the principles of sinful selfishness from the soul—to produce a spirit of meekness and self-denial, of readiness to forgive real injuries, and of prayer for the good of our enemies. Yes, the spirit of the gospel is love to God and to man, evidencing its existence by suitable exertions for the glory of our Creator, and the happiness of all our brethren, here and hereafter.

How does this system, Christian, correspond with the slave trade? You behold your African brethren in the same miserable state in which you are yourself by nature.* Do you not sympathize with them? Your Maker has not excluded them from a share in His love, nor has the blessed Redeemer interdicted them from claiming a share in His salvation. How can you degrade them, therefore, from that rank which their Maker has assigned to them, and endeavor to assimilate them to the beasts that perish? By divine grace you are taught not to love this world, nor to be conformed to its sinful practices. Rom. xii. 2. Look at your slave! How came you by him? Who had a right to tear his father from the bosom of his friends, in order to enslave him and his offspring, and sell this wretched victim to you? How long will religion suffer you to retain him in bondage? For life? Ah! hard-hearted Christian! is it thus you imitate His example who died for your sins? who voluntarily descended from His heavenly glory, and humbled Himself into the death, in order to deliver you from slavery? On Him rested the Spirit of the Lord, for He preached glad tidings unto the meek. He proclaimed liberty to the captive and the opening of the prison doors to them who were bound. Isa. lxi. 1. Does the same spirit rest on you? does it produce a similar disposition? Consider the contrast: consider it attentively. You have pronounced heavy tidings in the ear of your slave. You have proclaimed bondage for life to the captive. You have even closed upon him the door of hope in his prison. You have purposed to enslave his off-

Eph. ii. 3.

spring. Merciful God! how unmerciful do Thy creatures act towards one another?

6. The last argument I shall use for confirming the doctrine of the proposition, shall be taken from the pernicious consequences of the system of slavery.

To this manner of reasoning there can be no valid objection, if it be kept within proper boundaries. That evil consequences follow a certain practice is not always a decisive evidence that the practice is wrong; but it is a sufficient reason for us to pause, and examine it in the light of truth. If we be required, in the divine law, to pursue this path, we must obey, leaving the consequences to His management who commands us. If it be in itself lawful, but not requisite, evil consequences presenting themselves would teach us not to proceed. But if it really be a forbidden path, the pernicious effects of travelling it are additional warnings against continuing in it any longer.

Ministers are commanded to preach the gospel, though it should prove the occasion of submitting many to tribulation in this life, and be to many a *savor of death unto death in the next.* It was lawful for the apostle to the Gentiles to *eat whatsoever meat was sold in the shambles;* but if his using this liberty would have been productive of evil consequences, he would have instantly desisted from the practice. 1 Cor. viii. 13.

If, then, from a lawful practice, it be expedient to desist, because, although to ourselves useful, it is detrimental to others, it is certainly our duty to relinquish a system which is dubious in its nature. When we have presumptive evidence that we are fundamentally wrong, evil consequences are decisive against us; and, as in the case before us, when other evidences condemn the practice, its pernicious consequences loudly demand that from it we should immediately desist.

1. This practice has a tendency to destroy the finer feelings, and render the heart of man more obdurate. The butcher, long inured to slaughter, is not hurt at the lowing of the oxen, or the bleating of the lambs which he is about to kill.* Nor is the common executioner much agitated in his work of blood, whether the victim be innocent or guilty. The slave may roar under the lash of his master, without commanding the least sympathy. The slave-holder views all the Ethiopian race as born to serve. His heart is steeled against them. Nor is the transition great to become hard-hearted to all men. "The whole commerce between master and slave is a perpetual exercise of the most boisterous passions—the most unremitting despotism on the one part, and degrading submission on the other. The parent storms—the child looks on, catches the lineaments of wrath, puts on the same airs in the circle of smaller slaves, gives loose to the worst of his passions; and thus nursed, educated, and daily exercised in tyranny, cannot but be stamped by it with odious peculiarities. The man must be a prodigy who can retain his manners and morals undepraved by such circumstances."†

2. It debases a part of the human race, and tends to destroy their intellectual and active powers. The slave, from his infancy, is obliged implicitly to obey the will of another. There is no circumstance which can stimulate him to exercise his own intellectual

* Frequent attendance in the slaughter-house is supposed calculated to blunt the feelings of humanity. By the laws of England, a butcher is not admitted to sit on a jury, lest he should not be sufficiently delicate in cases of life and death.

† Jefferson's Notes. Query XVIII.

powers. There is much to deter him from such exercise. If he think or plan, his thoughts and plans must give way to those of his master. He must have less depravity of heart than his white brethren, otherwise he must, under this treatment, become thoughtless and sullen. The energies of his mind are left to slumber. Every attempt is made to smother them. It is not surprising that such creatures should appear deficient in intellect.

Their moral principles also suffer. They are never cultivated. They are early suppressed. While young, the little tyrants of their master's family rule over them with rigor. No benevolent tie can exist between them. The slave, as soon as he can exercise his judgment, observes laws to protect the life, the liberty and the property of his master; but no law to procure these for him. He is private property. His master's will is his rule of duty. We have no right to expect morality or virtue from such an education and such examples.

3. Another evil consequence is the encouragement of licentiousness and debauchery.

The situation of the blacks is such as to afford every encouragement to a criminal intercourse. This is not confined to the blacks themselves, but frequently and shamefully exists between them and their masters. The lust of the master may be gratified and strengthened by intercourse with the slave, without fear of prosecution for the support of the offspring, or the character of the mother. The situation of these women admits of few guards to their chastity. Their education does not strengthen it. In the Southern States, illicit connection with a negro or mulatto woman is spoken of as quite a common thing. No reluctance, delicacy or shame appear about the matter. The number of mulattoes in the Northern States prove that this evil is also prevalent among their inhabitants. It is usually a concomitant of slavery.

4. This leads to a fourth lamentable consequence— the destruction of natural affection.

An irregular intercourse renders it difficult for the father to ascertain his proper offspring. Among the slaves themselves marriage is a slender tie. The master sells the husband to a distance from his wife, and the mother is separated from her infant children. This is a common thing. It must destroy, in a great measure, natural affection. Nor is the evil confined to the slaves. Their master, in this instance, exceeds them in hardness of heart. He sees his slave nursing an infant resembling himself in color and in features. Probably it is his child, his nephew, or his grand-child. He beholds such, however, not as relatives, but as slaves, and rejoices in the same manner that he does in viewing the increase of his cows or his horses.*

5. Domestic tyranny, which exists as a correlative to domestic slavery, is a nursery for civil tyrants. Powerful must be the force of other principles, and singular the combination of circumstances, which can render an advocate for domestic slavery a sincere

---

* "It is far from being uncommon to see a Southern gentleman at dinner, and his reputed offspring, a slave, waiting at the table. ' I myself,' says a gentleman of observation, ' saw two instances of this kind; and the company would very facetiously trace the features of the father and mother in the child, and very accurately point out their more characteristic resemblances. The fathers, neither of them, blushed, nor seemed disconcerted. They were called men of worth, politeness and humanity.' The Africans are said to be inferior, in point of sentiment and feeling, to white people. The African labors night and day to collect a small pittance to purchase the freedom of his child. The white man begets his likeness, and, with much indifference, sees his offspring in bondage and misery, and makes not one effort to redeem his own blood."—*Morse's Universal Geography*, p. 66.

friend of civil liberty. Is it possible? If he can buy, sell, and enslave for life, any individual of the human race, for no reason but self-interest, I should be unwilling to trust him with the affairs of a nation. Had he it in his power to do it with impunity, and did it appear conducive to his interest, or gratifying to his ambition, he would become as really a despot as the most arbitrary monarch.

6. This practice is calculated to bring down the judgments of God on societies and individuals.

The toleration of slavery is a national evil. It is the worst of robberies sanctioned by law. It is treason against Heaven—a conspiracy against the liberties of His subjects. If the Judge of all the earth shall do right, He cannot but punish the guilty.

Nations, as such, have no existence in a future state: they must expect national judgments in the present. Distributive justice will measure their punishment according to their criminality. O America, what hast thou to account for on the head of slavery! Thou alone, of all the nations now on the earth, didst commission thy delegates, in peace, and in security from the over-awing menaces of a tyrant, or of factions, to form thy Constitution. Thou didst possess, in a peculiar sense, the light of reason, of science, of revelation, of past argumentation, and of past experience. Thou hadst thyself formerly condemned the principle, and, in the most solemn manner, made an appeal to Heaven for the justice of thy cause. Heaven heard, and answered agreeably to thy wishes. Yet thou didst contradict a principle so solemnly asserted. Thou hast made provision for increasing the number and continuing the bondage of thy slaves. Thy judgments may tarry, but they will assuredly come.* Individuals are also in danger. Those who live "*without God in the world*" may have temporal judgments inflicted upon them for the part they have acted in the encouragement of slavery ;. but the time of retribution is in the world to come. Even real Christians, the guilt of whose sins is removed through the atonement of Jesus, but who have learned the way of the heathen so far as to confirm to the wicked practice of buying, selling and retaining slaves, have a right to expect severe corrections. Psalm lxxxix. 30

---

* The Declaration of Independence has these words: "We hold these truths to be self-evident—that all men are created equal—that they are endowed by their Creator with certain unalienable rights—that among these are life, liberty, and the pursuit of happiness—that to secure these rights, governments are instituted among men." The negroes are created equal with the whites according to this instrument. Their liberty is an unalienable right. But this nation has taken away this unalienable right from them. And although the nation declares that government is instituted to preserve this right, the government still continues to deprive them of it. The United States, according to the late census, taken in 1801, hold 875,626 of the human race in slavery. They have, even in the Constitution of the general government, twelve years after the Declaration of Independence, made provision for the increase of the number. Art. I. Sect. 9. "The migration or *importation* of such persons as any of the States now existing shall think proper to admit, shall not be prohibited by the Congress prior to the year 1808." They have thus, inconsistently, constitutionally authorized a continuance of the worst of robberies. Very few of the States have made any adequate provision for the emancipation of their slaves. But the State of South Carolina has exceeded her sister States in endeavors to perpetuate this impious practice. What language can express the political inconsistency of a people who have inserted in a republican constitution of government the following section? Constitution of South Carolina, Art. i. Sect. 6. "No person shall be eligible to a seat in the House of Representatives unless he is a free white man. If a resident in the election district, he shall not be eligible to a seat in the House of Representatives unless he be legally seized and possessed, in his own right, of a settled freehold estate of five hundred acres of land, and TEN NEGROES." To tolerate slavery is an evil of no small magnitude ; to give it a national recommendation is still more inexcusable; but to render it a condition without which no man can represent, in the legislature, the district in which he lives, exceeds anything on record in the annals of nations. This Constitution was adopted as late as the year 1790.

—32. In proportion as they have an opportunity of ascertaining duty, will their danger increase, unless they cheerfully sacrifice interest to it. He who knows his master's will, and doeth it not, shall be beaten with many stripes. Luke xii. 47. I speak to you who parley with this temptation—you who, in defiance of conviction, are determined to go on in the paths of self-interest. In this very path you may meet correction. Your treasures are not secure. There is a God; and while godliness continues to have *the promise of the life which now is, as well as that which is to come,*[*] those who continue to practise on the system of slavery may expect to suffer loss. Watch them close: they may one day elude your vigilance, and escape with your treasure. The enslaved Hebrews were allowed to escape with the jewels of the Egyptians. You may lose, in a similar manner, as much of your property as you have withheld from them of their earnings whom you retain in bondage. If not, God has it in his power to send mildew and blasting upon your crops—murrain and pestilence among your herds—until you sustain a greater loss than you would have suffered by giving liberty to your slaves. I should think it a favorable evidence, though not a conclusive argument, that God has a regard for you, if you are thus chastised for your oppression of your brethren. *But if ye be without chastisement, whereof all are partakers, then are ye bastards and not sons.*[†]

I have now finished what I designed to say in confirmation of the doctrine of the proposition, and shall proceed,

II. To refute objections offered to the principle I have been defending.

[*] 1 Tim. iv. 8. [†] Hebrews xii. 8.

It is not to be expected that every objection shall
now occur. Some that are made probably I never
heard; and some which I have heard may have escaped my recollection. I shall not. however, design-
edly evade any that has the appearance of argument.
I shall examine each in order to ascertain its full
value.

OBJECTION I. "Nature has made a distinction between man and man. One has stronger intellectual
powers than another. As physical strength prevails
in the subordinate ranks of creation. let superiority of
intellect preside among intelligent creatures. The
Europeans and their descendants are superior in this
respect to the Africans. These latter are. moreover,
in their own country, miserable. Their state is not
rendered worse by being enslaved. It is just for the
more intelligent to rule over the more ignorant, and
to make use of their services."

ANSWER. The distinctions which nature makes between man and man are probably not so great as
those which owe their existence to adventitious circumstances.

The inferiority of the blacks to the whites has been
greatly exaggerated.* Let the fact, however, be grant-

* There is no reason to suppose the blacks destitute of mental powers.
In some settlements in this State, particularly along the Mohawk, and
in Scoharie, the negroes, although slaves, are admitted to the privilege
of consultation with their masters about the manner of conducting their
labor. They live, comparatively, at ease and in plenty. They con-
sult about the management of the farm, and frequently convey the produce to the markets. The negroes, in these places, are as intelligent and
active as their masters, unless the latter have had signal advantages from
education, and associating with superior company.

The courage and skill of the negroes in war will no longer be disputed,
after their transactions in St. Domingo and Guadaloupe are known. And
great must be his prejudice who can deny to the black Toussaint the
qualifications of a warrior and a statesman.

The writings of *Phillis Wheatly* evince that negroes are not destitute

ed, and yet the inference which is the principle of the objection will not follow. It is the essence of tyranny. It is founded in false notions concerning the nature of man. You say, "a greater proportion of intellect gives a right to rule over the less intelligent." But you are to observe that man is not only a creature capable of intellectual exertion, but also one who possesses moral sentiments, and a free agent. He has a right, from the constitution given him by the Author of Nature, to dispose of himself, and be his own master in all respects, except in violating the will of Heaven. He naturally acts agreeably to the motives presented to him, with a liberty of choice respecting them. He who argues a right to rule from natural endowments must have more than a superior understanding to show. He must evidence a superiority of moral excellence, and an investiture with authority; otherwise he can have no right to set aside the principle of self-government, and act in opposition to that freedom which is necessarily implied in personal responsibility to the Supreme Moral Governor. Consider the consequences which the objection, if granted, would involve. He who could, by cunning contrivance, reduce his innocent and more simple neighbor under his power, would be justifiable in enslaving him and his offspring for ever. All the usurpation of men of genius without virtue, from the days of Pharaoh to

of poetic genius; and the letters of *Ignatius Sancho* discover their possession of talents for prose composition. The observations of the Rev. Samuel Miller, of New York, on the negro school of that city, and those of Anthony Benezet on the school in Philadelphia, confirm this truth. But if any person desires more documents to corroborate the position that the talents of the negroes are not inferior to those of the whites, I refer him to Clarkson's Essay, and to Dr. Beattie's refutation of Hume's assertions with respect to African capacity. There he will find satisfaction.

those of Bonaparte, would be justifiable on this principle.

As for the circumstance of the Africans being wretched while at their own disposal, you are not accountable for it. Friendship for them is not well shown in the slave trade. Your wicked traffic has already rendered them more wicked and wretched even in Africa. If you have ameliorated the condition of one, you have rendered more painful the condition of thousands.*

Objection II. "The negroes are a different race of people from us. Their capacities, their shape, their color, and their smell, indicate their procedure originally from a different pair. They are inferior to the white people in all these respects. This gives a right to the superior race to rule over them as really as nature

* The nations called civilized, upon accurate calculation, are found to export annually from Africa *one hundred thousand* slaves. Fifty thousand of these are obtained by kidnapping. In order to supply the other half, whole villages are at once depopulated, by order of the Princes under European influence, and wars entered into expressly for the purpose of making slaves of the prisoners. These causes produce constant quarrels, and render the country miserable. It is supposed that 60,000 lives perish annually in these wars. Of the number shipped from Africa, 25,000 perish on the passage, by pestilence, insurrection, shipwreck, despair, &c. 25,000 more perish in seasoning to the climate of the West Indies. The remaining 50.000 linger out a life of wretched existence. Another fact will ascertain the havoc which famine, fatigue and cruelty make among those who are seasoned to the climate. Ten thousand people, under fair advantages, should produce, in a century, 160,000. In one of the colonies 650,000 slaves were imported in one century. The offspring of these, at the expiration of a hundred years, amounted to 140,000. According to this estimate, population was impeded in the proportion of seventy-four to one. In their own country they would have produced ten millions in that time. Thus it appears that upwards of 100,000 lives are annually sacrificed. This estimate is founded upon the testimony of witnesses by no means partial to the Africans—the testimonies of Smyth, Bosman, and Moore, agents to the factories established in Africa—and the records of Jamaica and St. Domingo. In Part III. of Clarkson's Essay, a history of the slave trade is given, and many tales of woo related. If the accuracy of this estimate is doubted, that excellent work may be consulted.

gives a right to the use of the other subordinate ranks of animated being."

ANSWER. This goes upon the footing of discrediting Scripture authority. In a discourse to professed Christians I might reject it without consideration There may, however, be in my hearing a slave-holder who is an unbeliever of revelation. I would reason even with him, that, if possible, I may serve the cause of justice, of liberty, and of man. The use of sound reason and philosophy Christianity by no means discards.

The principle of your argument is inadmissible ; and. if it were not, it would not serve your purpose.

1. It is inadmissible. Among the individuals of every species there is a difference. No more causes than are sufficient to account for any phenomenon are required by the rules of philosophising. The action of the elements on the human body, the diet and the manners of men, are causes sufficient to account for that change in the organization of bodies which gives them a tendency to absorb the rays of light, to perspire more freely, and to put on that shape which is peculiar to the inhabitants of Guinea and their descendants. A single century will make a forcible distinction between the inhabitants of a northern and a southern climate, when the diet and manners are similar. A difference in these can make a distinction in the same latitude. It is impossible to prove that twenty or thirty centuries, during which successive generations did not mingle with a foreign race, could not give to the African negro that peculiarity of bodily appearance which so stubbornly adheres to him when translated into another clime. A few years of a hot sun may produce a swarthiness of complexion which the mildest climate cannot, for years, exchange for a rosy cheek.

According to the laws for propagating the species, the offspring resembles the parent. It is not to be expected that a very apparent change should be wrought on the complexion of the offspring of negroes already in this country. Ten times the number of years which have passed over the heads of the successive generations on the coast of Guinea, may be necessary, before the negroes can retrace the steps by which they have proceeded from a fair countenance to their present shining black. The causes of bodily variety in the human species which I have stated are known to exist.* It is highly unphilosophical to have recourse to others which are only conjectural. Enmity to revelation makes many one think himself a philosopher. But,

2. If the principle were just it would be invalid: it would not answer your purpose. If you adopt the hypothesis of several original and distinct pairs, by whom the earth was peopled, you cannot determine where to stop. The different nations of Europe and of Asia, and the different tribes of America, may have had different original parents, all upon the footing of subordination one to the other.† If the principle of

* The author embraces this opportunity of recommending "An inquiry into the Causes of Variety in the Human Complexions," by Dr. Smith, President of the College of New-Jersey. His admirable criticisms on Lord Kaimes, by far the most able advocate of the doctrine of a plurality of distinct original pairs, deserve the perusal of the philosophic inquirer.

† Mr. Miller eloquently expresses himself on this subject:—"Pride, indeed, may contend that these unhappy subjects of our oppression are an inferior race of beings; and are, therefore, assigned, by the strictest justice, to a depressed and servile station in society. But in what does this inferiority consist? In a difference of *complexion and figure?* Let the narrow and illiberal mind, who can advance such an argument, recollect whither it will carry him. In traversing the various regions of the earth, from the equator to the pole, we find an infinite diversity of shades in the complexion of men, from the darkest to the fairest hues. If, then, the

your objection were admissible, it would prove too much, lead to absurdity, and is therefore capable of proving nothing. Each nation might claim a superiority of rank over the other. Right would be opposed to right, and cunning and violence would be the only umpires. Involve not yourself in such inextricable difficulties in advocating a practice truly indefensible.

Objection III. " I firmly believe the Scriptures. All the families of the earth are brethren. They are originally descended from Adam, and secondarily from Noah. But the blacks are the descendants of Ham. They are under a curse, and a right is given to their brethren to rule over them. We have a divine grant, in Gen. ix. 25—27, to enslave the negroes."

Answer. This threatening may have extended to all the descendants of Ham. It is, however, to be noticed, that it is directed to Canaan, the son of Ham. In order to justify negro slavery from this prophecy, it will be necessary to prove four things. 1. That all the posterity of Canaan were devoted to suffer slavery. 2. That African negroes are really descended of Canaan. 3. That each of the descendants of Shem and Japheth has a moral right to reduce any of them to servitude. 4. That every slave-holder is really descended from Shem or Japheth. Want of proof in any one of these particulars will invalidate the whole objection. In a

proper station of the African is that of servitude and depression, we must also contend that every Portuguese and Spaniard is, though in a less degree, inferior to us, and should be subject to a measure of the same degradation, Nay, if the tints of colour be considered the test of human dignity, we may justly assume a haughty superiority over our southern brethren of this continent, and devise their subjugation. In short upon this principle, where shall liberty end ? or where shall slavery begin ? at what grade is it that the ties of blood are to cease ? and how many shades must we descend still lower in the scale, before mercy is to vanish with th·m ."—*Discourse to the Manumission Society of New-York*, p. 12, 13.

practice so contrary to the general principles of the
divine law, a very express grant from the supreme authority is the only sanction to us. But not one of the
four facts specified as necessary can be supported with
unquestionable documents. On each of them, however, we may spend a thought.

1. The threatening is general. It does not imply particular personal servitude as much as political inferiority and national degradation. It does not imply that
every individual of that race should of right be kept
in a state of slavery.

2. It is possible the negroes are descended from Ham.
It is even probable. But is almost certain that they are
not the offspring of Canaan. The boundaries of their
habitation are defined. Gen. x. 19. The Canaanitish
territory is generally known from subsequent history.

3. The supposition, however, that the curse fell on
the negroes, may be granted with safety to the cause
of those who are opposed to the system by which they
are enslaved. It will not serve as a warrant for this
practice. It is not to be considered as a rule of duty,
but as the prediction of a future event. God has, in
his providence, given many men over to slavery, to
hardships, and to death. But this does not justify the
tyrant and the murderer. Had it been predicted, in
so many words, that the Americans should, in the be-
ginning of the nineteenth century, be in possession of
African slaves, we might argue from the fact the truth
of the prophecy, but not the propriety of the slave-
holder's conduct. It was foretold that Israel should
be in bondage in Egypt. Gen. xv. 13. This did not
justify the cruelty of Pharaoh. He was a vessel of
wrath. Jesus, our God and Redeemer, was the subject of many predictions. According to ancient prophecy, and to satisfy divine justice, he was put to death.

The characters who fulfilled this prediction were wicked to an extreme. Acts ii. 23.

4. Slave-holders are probably the descendants of Japheth, although it cannot be legally ascertained. And they may be fulfilling the threatening on Canaan, although they are not innocent. Be not afraid, my friends; prophecy shall be fulfilled, although you should liberate your slaves. This prediction has had its accomplishment three thousand years ago. The descendants of Shem did, by divine direction, under the conduct of Joshua, subjugate the offspring of Canaan, when they took possession of the promised land.

This naturally leads to consider another objection—the most plausible argument that can possibly be offered in defence of the unhallowed practice of holding our fellow men in perpetual bondage.

OBJECTION IV. "God permitted the ancient Israelites to hold their fellow creatures in servitude. Men and women were bought and sold among them. The bond servant is called his master's money. Exod. xxi. 21. Had it been wrong in its nature to enslave any human being, God could not have granted the Hebrews a permission to do it. Negro slavery, stripped of some accidental cruelties, it is not necessarily wicked."

ANSWER. This objection requires minute attention. The fact is granted. Heaven did permit the Hebrews to purchase some of the human race for servitude. The general principle deduced from this fact is also granted. It is, in certain cases, lawful to enslave our fellow creatures. The application of it to justify the practice of modern nations is by no means admissible.

God is the Lord of the universe. As the Supreme Governor, he does what is right. His subjects have violated his law, abused their liberty, and rebelled

against the majesty of Heaven. They have forfeited
to his justice the liberty and the life he gave them.
These they must yield. They will, at the time appointed by the Judge, be enclosed in the grave. The
sovereign has also a right to the use of whatever instrument he chooses in the execution of the sentence. He
may choose the famine or the pestilence, the winds or
the waves, wild beasts or human beings, to be the executioners. Again:

Civil society has certain laws, to which its members,
voluntarily claiming its privileges, have assented.
A violation of these is a violation of a contract, and
the penalty stipulated must be paid by the offender.
When, by a person's licentiousness, justice is violated,
or society endangered, it is just and necessary to enslave
the criminal, and make his services, if possible, useful
to society. This much I cheerfully grant; and shall
now proceed to show that the objection does not apply to the doctrine which I have been endeavouring
to establish.

You cannot argue conclusively, in defence of negro
slavery, from the practice of the ancient Hebrews, unless you can prove, 1st. That the slavery into which
they were permitted to reduce their fellow creatures
was similar to that in which the negroes are held:
and, 2dly. That you have, the same permission which
they had, extended to you. If proof fails in *either* of
these, the objection is invalid, and I undertake to show
that *both* are without proof.

I. The servitude into which the Hebrews were permitted to reduce their fellow men was attended with
such restrictions as rendered it essentially different from
the negro slave trade. It may be considered, 1. With
reference to their brethren; 2. As it respected strangers

1. A natural descendant of Abraham might, in two cases, be sold by the magistrates into servitude. These were theft and insolvency. And so great was the regard for freedom which their code of laws discovered, that even the thief could not be enslaved while he had property sufficient to answer the demands of the law for the theft, Exod. xxii. 1—4. *If a man shall steal an ox or a sheep, and kill it, or sell it, he shall restore five oxen for the ox, and four sheep for the sheep. If a thief have nothing, then he shall be sold for his theft.* The servitude into which the debtor was sold for the benefit of the creditor was not severe. Lev. xxv. 39—43. *If thy brother that dwelleth with the be waxen poor, and be sold unto thee, thou shalt not compel him to serve as a bond servant, but as an hired servant and as a sojourner he shall be with thee. Thou shalt not rule over him with rigour, but shalt fear thy God.* In both cases the duration of this species of slavery was limited to six years. *On the seventh he shalt go out free for nothing.* Exod. xxi. 2. And it was required, in the case of the debtor, that his master should give him some stock on which he might again begin business for the support of his family. Deut. xv. 12—15. *When thou sendest him out free, thou shalt furnish him liberally of thy flock, thy flour, and thy wine-press.*

Both these laws evidence the greatest care of the liberties of individuals which is consistent with the real interest of the nation. They are strong motives to industry, and guard against burdensome taxation for the support of prisons.

2. There were two classes of aliens with respect to which the Israelitish law gave directions—those who belonged to any of the neighboring Camaanitish tribes in particular, and such as belonged to other nations in general. With respect to the latter, the law was ex-

actly the same as to the Hebrews themselves. Lev. xxiv. 22. *Ye shall have one manner of law as well for the stranger as for one of your own country.* Verse 35, next chapter. *If thy brother be waxen poor, then thou shalt relieve him—yea, though he a stranger or a sojourner.* But there are particular exceptions from this general law, which guaranteed from invasion the life, the liberty, and the property of aliens. These exceptions refer to the remains of the conquered tribes living among the Israelites, or to such of the nations of Canaan as were around them. Lev. xxv. 44,45. *Of the heathen that are round about you, shall ye buy bondmen and bondmaids. Of the children of the strangers that sojourn among you, shall ye buy, and of the families which they begat in your land.* This permission was merciful. The descendants of Abraham were expressly appointed the executioners of the divine sentence against the tribes of Canaan. Extermination was the command ; but on their voluntary subjection they were only reduced into a state of servitude. The Israelites were forbidden to use them harshly. Exod. xxi. 26. Accordingly, the Gibeonites, when they craftily obtained the safety of their lives, were reduced into the situation of bond servants. Joshua ix. When Saul treated them with cruelty, God was offended, and even punished David because he did not avenge that cruelty on the house of Saul, at an early part of his reign. 2 Sam. xxi. 1, I proceed,

II. To prove that this example is not for our imitation. The Israelites themselves had no right to fit out their ships with their implements of cruelty, in order to steal, buy, stow away, and chain men of other nations, living, without injury to them, at a distance from their shores. Had they done so, no future traffic could have rendered their prizes legitimate. They were officially employed by Heaven to punish the iniquity of the nations which they vanquished. They were ordered to subdue, destroy or enslave the descendants of Canaan, and take possession of the land covenanted to their father Abraham. As a peculiar people, they were to be kept distinct until Messiah should come. The remains of foreign nations could not, therefore, be admitted to the rights of citizenship. The wall of partition is now broken down. All mankind are our brethren. There is no similarity of circumstances between us and the ancient Hebrews—no divine permission that can justify us in holding slaves. Although the slavery were exactly the same with that into which the blacks are reduced, the practice of modern nations would remain unjustifiable.

The decendants of Shem have, in the Hebrew nation, reduced Canaan into a state of servitude ; and the offspring of Japheth have surplanted those of Shem in both spiritual and temporal privileges.

OBJECTION V. "Slavery was tolerated, in primitive ages of Christianity, by the Roman laws. It is not condemned by Christ or his Apostles. They have given directions for the conduct of master and slave. 1 Tim. vi. 1. They have not intimated that the practice of keeping men in slavery was sinful."

ANSWER. What you have asserted is not correct, and, if it had been, it would be no objection to the principles for which I contend. The New Testament does condemn the slave-trade. 1 Tim. i. 10. *Man stealing* is here reprobated, together with every practice which is contrary to *sound doctrine* and the spirit of the *glorious gospel.* 1 Cor. vii. 21. *If thou mayest be made free, use it rather.* It is recommended to the slave, if he is able, to procure his liberty. If he

has no fair means of obtaining it, it is his duty patient-
ly to continue in bondage.* The gospel hope comforts
him. The New Testament says (Col. iv. 1.). *Masters,*

* Commerce in the human species is of a very early date. Moses informs us that Joseph was sold as a slave, and disposed of in Egypt as
such by the purchasers. Gen. xxxvii. 30, 36. Homer informs us, that
in the time of the Trojan war Egypt and Cyprus were markets for slaves.
Antinous threatens to send Ulysses to one of those places. Odys. lib.
XVII. v. 448.

Μη ταχα πικρην Αιγυπτον και Κυπρον ιδηαι.

Tyre and Sidon were notorious for prosecuting the slave trade. This
custom travelled over all Asia; spread through the Grecian and Roman world : and was practised among the barbarious nations which
overturned the Roman Empire. The abolition of the slave-trade among
the European nations has been falsely attributed to the feudal system.
The prevalence of Christianity was the real cause of it. The charters
which were granted, in those days, for the freedom of slaves, were expressly, *pro amore Dei, pro mercede animæ* ; " that they might procure
the favour of the Deity, which they conceived themselves to have forfeited by the subjugation of those whom they found to be the objects of divine benevolence." These effects were produced as the nations were
converted, and procured a general liberty through Europe before the
close of the twelfth century. In the commencement of this century slaves
were a capital article in the domestic and foreign trade of England. When
any person had more children than he could maintain, he sold them to
a merchant. In the council held at St. Peters, Westminster. A. D. 1102,
this practice was prohibited. In the great Council of Armagh, A. D. 1171,
the clergy of Ireland decreed that all the English slaves should be immediately emancipated. (*Henry's England,* vol. vi. p. 267, 8vo. edit.) It
had not yet been discovered that the New Testament authorised slavery.
No. Wherever this religion prevails, it will be found to be the "*perfect
law of liberty.*"

The instance of Onesimus has been very unhappily selected by the
advocates of slavery to support their system. It does not appear certainly that he had been a slave to Philemon. He had been, indeed, a servant.
But, if a slave, he was to be so no longer. Phil. 16. Paul had a right to
demand his liberty. Phil. 8. He knows, however, that to request it
would be sufficient. Phil. 9. It appears Onesimus had wronged his
master. Phil. 18. Notwithstanding, Paul might lawfully have retain-
ed him without a recompence. Phil. 13. But, confiding in Philemon's
integrity, leaves the matter to his own option, and becomes security for
Onesimus. Phil. 15. It appears that this Onesimus was no longer slave
or servant. He was more probably afterwards a minister of the gospel,
and colleague with Tychicus in Collosse. He is said to have been afterwards pastor at Ephesus.

give unto your servants that which is just and equal.
Treat them justly; use them mercifully; pay them lawful wages; give them an epuivalent for their services. But, supposing the Scriptures had been silent on this subject, the objector could not justify negro slavery from that silence. If it prove anything it will prove too much. It will prove the justice of the worst of tyranny, the most dreadful cruelty, because Nero is not specified as an infamous tyrant in the New Testament. It will prove that you have a right to sell your own children as slaves*—to kidnap your neighbor, your countryman and your friend. You need not, therefore, confine your traffic in human flesh to the African race. You may extend it even to your own children. But if such practices are not formally mentioned and condemned in the New Testament, the principles from which they proceed are reprobated in the strongest terms. The whole system of slavery is opposite to the spirit of that religion which is righteousness and peace. True religion cheers the heart both of the subject of a tyrant and the slave of a master. It teaches them their duty as men, as social beings, as citizens of the world; while it reprobates the character who holds them in durance, and condemns the tenor upon which he holds his authority. It does not alter the external condition of the believer, unless it teaches the heart of those who are in power. It teaches him faithfulness and sobriety, patience and resignation, until God, in his providence, affords him an opportunity of being more usefully active in the restoration of moral order to society.

---

* The immoralities practised in the Roman Empire, under the sanction of law, were numerous and aggravated. It would be an unreasonable mode of compiling a system of ethics, to sustain as moral every ancient usage of the Grecians and Romans which are not expressly condemned in the New Testament.

OBJECTION VI. "I abhor the principle. The practice of importing and selling men is detestable. But here they are. We found them slaves. We are not obliged, at the expense of our property, to set them at liberty. The community in general will not consent to it. They will therefore be slaves. I want a servant. I may purchase and hold a slave. His condition will not be rendered worse by serving me. I am bound to treat him mercifully: but, as matters are now situated, there can be no evil in my keeping him in bondage."

ANSWER. If men were not strongly influenced by interested motives, they could not impose so far on their own understandings as to give indulgence to the principle contained in this objection. *A long continuance of evil doing will change the nature of wrong into right.* If so, there is an end to the distinction between virtue and vice. Your fathers left the negroes in bondage, as an inheritance to you. Does this justify you in retaining them? No. If the first stealer and the first buyer acted contrary to justice, the constant retainer cannot be guiltless. You condemn the principle, but justify the practice. Act consistently, I beseech you. *Touch not, taste not, handle not the unclean thing.* Let me call your attention to another fact. You have a slave of thirty years of age in your possession. He was born in your house. By natural laws, and according to the first principles of civil liberty, he was born equally free with your son. Who has, upon him, committed the robbery by which he has been deprived of his natural rights? Yourself. Lay not the blame on your parents; for you imitate their example. The text applies to you directly. You have stolen from his connections, from himself, a man born in your house. Have you purchased him?

You have contenanced an impious commerce; the best reparation you can make is to set your slave at liberty. You cannot afford to perform acts of such extensive benevolence. Do justice, however. Deal mercifully with your servant. When the wages which he might have annually earned shall have amounted to the purchase money, and lawful interest, set him immediately at liberty from your controul. If you are a worthy character, he shall afterwards voluntarily serve you, unless he be ungrateful indeed, provided you give him due wages. After confessing the system to be indefensible, it is to be hoped you will not give your suffrages to render it permanent..—I shall proceed,

III. To make some improvement.

In his walk of faith, the Christian considers himself bound to the practice of every known duty. By the test of obedience, the nature of his love to God is tried. *This is the love of God, that ye keep his commandments, and his commandments are not grievous.** This disposition inclines and fits him for making a practical improvement of just theory. And the view we have now had of the evils of the slave-trade may be improved for several uses.

1. We should lament over the distressing sufferings of our brethren in bondage. True piety does not blunt the feelings of benevolence. Commiseration with the wretched is strongly inculcated. *Weep with those that weep.* Evangelic principle forms the soul to it. *For these things I weep: mine eye, mine eye, runneth down with tears.*† The situation of the African is miserable. In his native country he is in darkness. He has no vision, no well grounded hope—the inhabi-

* Rom. xii. 15.   † Lament. i. 16.

tant of a waste wilderness, without God in the world.
He becomes acquainted with foreigners on whom a
Christian education has been bestowed. They profess
the religion which breathes peace and good will towards men. He knows them to his sorrow. New
occasions for war are afforded, and new and terrible
instruments for prosecuting war provided, for the already ferocious tribes of the wilderness. He is taken
captive, and is sold for a bauble. He is chained in
the suffocating dungeon of a floating prison. He is
brought into a strange country. The whip is brandish-
ed over his head. With its lash his back is furrowed.
In a land boasting of civilization, and enlightened by
the gospel luminary, he is doomed to ignorance, to
rudeness and wretchedness. *There is power on the
side of the oppressor, but on his side there is no power.* *
His genius is cramped; the energy of his mind are
suppressed; his moral feelings are eradicated; his
soul, his immortal soul, is left to perish without the
knowledge of Jesus. " Oh, slavery, thou art a bitter
draught!" Miserable African, we lament over your
condition. We are sensible of your sufferings. We
sympathise with you. We recognise you as a brother.
We recommend you to the protection of our Heavenly
Father. We consign you to the arms of our dear
Redeemer. God of mercy! *Let the sighing of the
prisoner come before thee: according to the greatness
of thy power, preserve thou those that are appointed
to die.* †

2. We may improve the view we have taken of the
negro slave-trade, in order to stimulate us to present
duty.

The benevolence of the Christian is not like the sen-

* Eccles. iv. i.   † Psalm lxxix. ii.

sibility of a writer of romance, ready to be exercised on imaginary objects, but blind to objects of reality. While we drop the tear of compassion over the slave, let us enquire whether or not we can do anything to alleviate his sorrows. Cannot your agency diminish the number of slaves, and your behavior be an example to others to contribute their influence to the same desirable end?

I cannot demand of you, my brethren, to sacrifice your property imprudently in purchasing the liberty of your neighbour's slaves; but justice, your religion, requires that you should cease to be slave-holders yourselves. With respect to the young, arrangements may be made, to defray, by their services, the expense of their support and their education, before they are emancipated. To this you have a right, and to no more. The middle-aged has already repaid your expenditures. If he has been purchased, charity would recommend it to you, nevertheless, to set him at liberty: and justice demands that you should retain him in bondage no longer than is sufficient to recompence you for your trouble and expense. With reference to the old, the inactive and the infirm, Godly wisdom will direct the conscientious to such measures as may be best calculated to secure their advantage, and enable you to maintain an honourable testimony against this abominable usurpation. Be merciful to them. Cultivate their understandings. Make them feel themselves to be men. Raise them to the rank which God has assigned them. Teach them the doctrines of the gospel. Give them habits of industry. Pray for them. Sacrifice the property which the civil law gives you in them, on the altar of religion. Seek for a recompense from on high. Heaven can reward you. *Godliness* *is profitable unto all things. It has the promise of the life which now is, and of that which is to come.**

3. The preceding discussion may be improved for discovering the duty of gospel ministers.

These occupy an important office in the house of God. They are embassadors for Jesus Christ. They are commissioned not so much to please as to teach. The volume of revelation contains their instructions. In negociating a treaty between heaven and earth, they are not to neglect its directions. It contains no useless articles to be expunged or neglected. Much prudence, much prayer, and large communications of the divine spirit, are indeed necessary to constitute fallible man a wise steward of the manifold grace of God. This is promised; *and he is faithful who promised, and able to perform.†* Mankind have no right to be offended at ministers for directing them on the head of slavery. My text is in the Bible. I have an undoubted right to discuss it. Is the discussion scriptural, and is it well timed? are the only questions men have a right to ask. My brethren in the ministry, if you lament over this evil, let your voice be raised aloud against it. The subject is important. To handle it rashly may be dangerous. Offence may be undesignedly given, and unjustly taken, which may mar the peace of the church, and hinder the propagation of the of the gospel. *Offences must come.* Woe to him by whom they are introduced. This should make you vigilant, but not silent. Some, indeed, have pushed their opposition to political evils too far. This may have had an influence in deterring others from going as far as duty directed. There is a timidity natural to some characters, which detains them from prosecuting

* 1 Tim. iv. 8.   † Heb. x. 2, 3.   Ro n. iv. 21.

public subjects. Some, who are traitors to their Master's cause, neglect some articles in their instructions, while negociating in his name; and there is a meekness and diffidence cherished by true piety, which render ministers more disposed to evangelic discussions than to inveigh against public immoralities. But remember, brethren, that in preaching the gospel you are not to neglect the law. *It is to be used as a schoolmaster to lead men to Christ, who is the end of the law for righteousness to every one who believeth.* And you are also to teach, that the gospel is designed to establish the law, and dispose men to obey its dictates. You may comfort yourselves, probably, while neglecting your duty upon such subjects, by classing yourselves with an apostle, in desiring to *know nothing but Jesus, and him crucified.* Be assured, however, that the resolution of that inspired writer was not recorded with a view to militate against the express precept of our arisen Lord. He commanded his ambassadors not only to *preach the gospel to all nations,* but also to *teach them all things whatsoever he commanded.** Considering the guilt and the danger accompanying the practice of holding our brethren in perpetual slavery, it will be serving God in your generation prudently to exercise the right of giving public warning against it. Let us do our duty, leaving the consequences to God.

4. The view we have taken of this subject also affords a practical lesson to our legislators and statesmen. To you belongs the maintenance of justice and order in society. Your influence, your authority, your wisdom, can be of signal service to the nation, if they are all exerted in the cause of righteousness. Engage yourself speedily in rectifying this evil practice of holding

* Matt. xxviii. 19, 20.

your brethren in slavery. It is inconsistent with the
natural rights of man; it is condemned by the Scriptures; it is at war with your republican institutions;
it ruins the minds and the morals of thousands; and
it leaves you exposed to the wrath of heaven. It is
easy to see that, although it supports indolence and
the pride of families, it is truly detrimental to the
wealth, the industry, the population, and the safety
of the commonwealth.* It may be difficult to point
out a safe mode of redressing the evil. Every plan is
accompanied with difficulties. To export them to
Africa would be cruel. To establish them in a separ-
ate colony would be dangerous. To give them their
liberty, and incorporate them with the whites, would

---

* "From repeated and accurate calculations, it has been found that
the expense of maintaining a slave, if we include the purchase-money,
is much greater than that of maintaining a free man; and the labor of
the free man, influenced by the powerful motive of gain, is at least
twice as profitable to the employer as that of the slave. Besides, slavery is the bane of industry. It renders labor among the whites not
only unfashionable, but disreputable. Industry is the offspring of necessity rather than of choice. Slavery precludes this necessity, and
indolence, which strikes at the root of all social and political happiness, is the consequence." *Morse's Geography, p.* 65.

If these observations be just, it appears that slavery is impolitic as
well as immoral; and they will hold true except in cases in which the
negroes are treated in some degree as men, and in which they enjoy a
considerable portion of freedom: and even where this is the case, there
is a great disadvantage accompanying negro slavery. It renders service
of any kind disreputable. All the white people cannot be masters, and
yet even the poor are very unwilling to serve. When they do engage
in service it is difficult to deal with them. If you assume an authority
over them they resent it; if you have work to do which is disagreeable,
your hired man or woman spurn at the thought of being more meanly
employed than yourself; nay, they will not be called servants, for this
would be reducing them to a level with the blacks. This is prevalent
throughout the country, except in those places in which different cus-
toms have introduced different ideas. The want of subordination and
faithfulness in the white servants in America, has long been a subject
of remark to Europeans. In the slavery of the blacks we see the cause
of it—a cause more powerful than even mistaken notions of liberty.

be more so. The sins of the fathers, it is to be feared, will be visited on their children. But it is more safe to adopt any one of those plans than continue the evil. By a national repenting and forsaking, we may find mercy. Providence can dispose of all things in our favor. We have a right to expect that He will ward off or mitigate the threatening consequences, if the nation would venture upon His kindness to do their duty.

It must appear ridiculous to Europeans "to hear of an American patriot signing with one hand declarations of independency, and with the other brandishing a whip over an affrighted slave." Can you be sincere friends to liberty and order, and tolerate this dreadful traffic.

From repeated and accurate calculations, it has been found that slavery is unfavorable to the wealth of nations.

Listen to the remarks of a writer of observation and eminence. "With what execration should the statesman be loaded, who, permitting one half of the citizens thus to trample on the rights of the other, transforms those into despots, and these into enemies —destroys the morals of the one part, and the *amor patriæ* of the other! With the morals of the people, their industry also is destroyed. Of the proprietors of slaves a small proportion is ever seen to labor. And can the liberties of a nation be thought secure, when we have removed their only firm basis, a conviction in the minds of the public that their liberties are the gift of God? that they are not to be violated but with his wrath? Indeed, I tremble for my country when I reflect that God is just—that his justice cannot sleep for ever—that an exchange of situation is among possible events—that it may become probable by supernatural interference."* You will find it true, *that righteousness exalteth a nation, and that sin is a reproach to any people.*†

In concluding this discourse, let me warn my hearers to consider the evil hand they may have in the system of slavery, and especially that they are by nature in the worst of slavery themselves. Come for deliverance from the bondage of sin unto the Son of God: for, *whom the Son makes free, shall be free indeed.* Standing fast in this liberty, use it in the service of God and of man. *You are no more your own; ye are bought with a price. Glorify God in your bodies and spirits which are his.* AMEN.

---

* Jefferson's Notes. † Prov. xiv. 34.

APPENDIX.

THE PRESENT WAR IMPROVED.

EXTRACTS FROM A SERMON PREACHED ON THANKSGIVING DAY, NOVEMBER 27, 1862, IN HIS CHURCH, BY JOHN N. McLEOD, D.D., NEW YORK.

THE REBELLION A MORAL WRONG.

The Southern insurrection which has precipitated us into war, is not only unconstitutional, inexpedient, and perilous to all the economical interests of the country, but also a great moral wrong,—a resistance to the ordinance of God which justly exposes to the merited condemnation. And hence too, with our ecclesiastical brethren all over the land, we have sustained the war, as a war of defence of God's ordinance of civil government, of the liberties of man, and of the religion of Jesus Christ. In this case emphatically the " Ruler " as God's " minister " should not bear the sword in vain. What is war but wholesale capital punishment? What is rebellion but the capital offence that authorises its infliction? We deplore the occasion, the fact, and the consequences of the existing war, as we would deplore the suffering which all punishment involves; but we would still call for its vigorous prosecution as the only means of restoring order, reforming wrong and re-establishing a righteous and permanent peace. We would do honor to the Christian ministers and other men who have gone out from our own Church, in the spirit of a noble ancestry, to fight the battles of their country. And we would inscribe the names of the many who have already fallen, on the same column that records and perpetuates the martyrdoms of the earlier times.

That nations as such are amenable to the law of God, and to punishment for its violation is a dictate of Bible morality which it is criminal to ignore. Existing only in the present life their retribution is here and now. As moral persons they are taught, warned, chastised; and reformed and spared, or utterly destroyed as they receive or reject the Divine admonitions. The past is full of examples of this. The prophetic history of the future recorded in the Apocalypse shows that there is more of it to come. And the wrecks of empires and republics which are scattered everywhere over the great ocean of time are startling evidences of its certainty and importance. For the nation and kingdom (says Isaiah) that will not serve thee shall perish; yea those nations shall be utterly wasted. This is the great lesson which God is teaching the American

Republic now. And every painful stroke which he inflicts upon her by the iron rod of war is either a prelude to destruction, or a prompter to repentance and reform. We yet believe that he who has sent it as a judgment from his own hand, will employ the war to bring us to the reformation which he demands.

THE SINS WHICH GOD IS REBUKING.

We do not now attempt to present a catalogue of the national sins which God is so severely rebuking. Among them are unboubtedly our pride and vain glory. This has offended God, and he is humbling us before other nations, and ourselves. And along with this we have to lament our ingratitude towards God, who has distinguished us by so many mercies; our intense worldliness as a great commercial people, our elevation of bad men to office and power, the terrible corruption that prevails in the management of public trusts, and of the public treasure, the Sabbath-breaking, profaneness, and infidel disregard of the law and religion of Jesus Christ which in practice produces no disqualification from office in the State; and in addition to all this, the encouragement and support which past administrations of the National Government have given to Southern slavery, and the growing despotism which it has created. We have always been among the number of those in our country who have regarded slavery, as it exists among us, as a local and not as a national institution; and that the ultimate responsibility for its evils rested upon the individual slaveholders themselves, and the State authorities to which they are more immediately subject. But this has not prevented us from seeing that the corrupting influence of this great iniquity has been constantly increasing and extending; that it has at last become a giant power in the land, and that with the one hand it was attempting to grasp the national sceptre, while with the other it was holding down in the dust of their degradation the increasing millions of its wronged and unhappy subjects. And the conclusion is evident, that while the South is more immediately and directly responsible for the wrong and evil of the bondage perpetuated among themselves; the North is also responsible for them before God, just so far as they are sustained by the opinion, sympathies and acts of individuals, and by the public deeds and policies of public men, and Federal laws, judgments, and administrations.

SLAVERY AND THE WAR.

And this is the moral connection which we perceive between Slavery and the War. God's forbearance with this evil here would seem to be exhausted, and he has come out of his place to punish the guilty. He is punishing the South with desolating armies, with a ruined commerce with a depreciated currency, with threatened famine, with alarms of servile war, with the destruction of her monuments of Family pride, and with the baptism of blood which her people are experiencing. And he is chastising the North with the same storm of bloody revolution, disturbing her industry, bringing uncertainty on her future, threatening the destruction of the Union to which she adheres, desolating her households, also, and exposing her to the peril of falling before her own divided and conflicting parties. In all this there is righteous retribution, and to perceive and profit by it is to take the first step to repentance, reform, and national salvation. We must by no means involve the whole country in equal guilt in regard to the evil of slavery. They who have always opposed and labored to remove it by the means provided by the Gospel may rejoice that they have in so far discharged their duty. The measure of chastisement which belongs to each is for the determination of Him who inflicts it.

EMANCIPATION SIXTY-THREE YEARS AGO.

When the Reformed Presbyterian Church, some sixty-three years ago, condemned the principle and practice of "holding unoffending men in bondage," (and this is her definition of Slavery,) she at the same time proclaimed emancipation of the bondmen of her members. They acquiesced, and the object was effected. Some of the men who witnessed the transaction have lived to see many of the other churches of the land coming up to the platform which she then occupied almost alone. And they have beheld the President of the United States issuing his proclamation for freedom, and in their supreme judicatory they have thanked him for it. They rejoice to see that the friends of emancipation are increasing by tens of thousands. That multitudes of the oppressed are gaining their freedom, and showing their ability to use and enjoy it; that the Christianity of the land is on their side, and that many of the slaveholders themselves are inquiring for a better way. In all this they see the morning star that is the harbinger of the coming day of universal liberty to man. Its radiance may be obscured by the war clouds among which it has arisen, but still it is there, and if it goes down, it will only be to give place to the sun in due season. There is no incongruity in the thoughts that the present war is at once the rod of God to break Slavery to pieces, and of paternal chastisement for the correction, reform, and salvation of our country.

OTHER ASPECTS OF THE CONFLICT.

And here also we see the present conflict in other of its higher aspects. Commenced and precipitated upon us by the slaveholding South, to sustain their secession, which is ultimate anarchy—on the part of the government of the Union it is a war of defence. They defend the law against treason, their property against wholesale plunder, their national life against the weapon of the assassin, and the principle of republican government itself against those who would bring it into contempt and shame. Nay more, the war is for liberty itself. The slavery of man by his fellow man is a violation of natural right. It is inconsistent with the genius of the Christian system. It is a painful degradation of its unhappy subject. It is a disturber of the whole order of society. It is a nurse of tyrants. It must therefore be in conflict with liberty and right wherever they co-exist, and the strife for the mastery must sooner or later come. Restrained, palliated, postponed, it has at last come among ourselves, and we are witnesses of it to-day. Leaving all the smaller questions involved to the economists and the politicians, we would desire to rise to the eminences of the subject, and be found on the side of liberty. We can be found nowhere else.

Nor can the result be doubtful. Let the Southern oligarchy be successful, and build up their social arch with slavery as its keystone, their triumph will be but temporary. The world, inconsistent as it is, will be against them. Their four millions of bondsmen cannot be kept in chains with freedom all around them, and war with other States and Nations will divide their strength and break their power, and God, who is the guardian of the oppressed, will not always suffer the wrongs done to his creatures. Let the Southern politicians be disappointed, their insurrection suppressed, and their social system revolutionized, and slavery will die the death. Let the war be stopped by the compromises of unprincipled politicians, and a re-adjustment leaving slavery where it was be effected, and even this is possible, and yet after all the triumph of oppression would be but evanescent. It is too late in the day of the world's progress to admit of its being lasting. The mass of the intelligence and the virtue of this nation have become persuaded that slavery is a wrong and a curse, and the cause of our present conflict in which the national life is endangered, and they will not rest under the distressing burden. The founders of the American Union never imagined that slavery would have lived till this hour of the day as a great disturbing power in the Republic. Let the burden be thrown off in season. It has been carried too long already. Let the Republic attempt to carry it no longer, lest sinking under its accumulated weight both fall together. But we confidently hope for better things than these. Let the nation return to God by adequate repentance of all its social sins. Let every yoke of oppression be broken ; let God and Jesus Christ his Son be honored by a due national acknowledgment ; let God's ordinance of civil order be administered by the Christian rule, and this great people will yet flourish in all that appertains to a Christian nation.

From Banner of the Covenant, February 11, 1860.

This remarkable discourse which was the first issue from the press, of its gifted author, is again presented to the public, by his grandson, and namesake in New York. It has been said of opinions and events, that they move in a circle. This sermon is an evidence of this. Though fifty-eight years old, its adaptations to present times, and to the new phases of the question of human liberty, appearing at present in our country, are most striking. When the Reformed Presbyterian Church assumed the ground which is maintained in this discourse, on the subject of slavery, she stood alone among the churches. At the expense of much self-denial by herself, and of much misconception and opposition by others, she has continued to maintain it to the present day; and she now sees whole communities in the Christian Church coming up to, and deliberately occupying with her the same platform. Treating the subject as a great question of moral duty, she has continued to tell her own people, her sister churches, and the great nation whose privileges she enjoys, that American Slavery is wrong, and that therefore every means consistent with the gospel, shou'd be used by church and state for its speedy removal from the land. She sympathizes with her brethren of the colored race, whether actually in bonds, or nominally free, and claims for the right to know and enjoy the gospel. She encourages no violent insurrections, or inconsiderate use of force, as a remedy for the evil, but seeks to apply the moral law, and the principles of the gospel to the case, that men may be pursuaded to do to their fellows in bonds, that which is just and equal, and thus break every yoke and set the oppressed free. The discourse before us is eminently scriptural, its ground is radical, its arguments are hard, its opinions are fearlessly uttered, but it comes to all in the spirit of Christian kindness, and with the persuasions of the gospel of Jesus Christ. No change has been made in any respect from the original; and it is commended to the perusal of all.

From National Standard, Feb. 2, 1860.

A VOICE FROM THE PAST.—This discourse was preached and first published fifty-eight years ago. The author was well-known in this city for many years, as an eloquent preacher, able theologian, and clear and earnest writer on moral and political topics. Having received a call, in November, 1800, to take the pastoral charge of a congregation in Orange County, and noticed among the signers some whom he knew to be slaveholders, he did not consent to accept the place until he had made known his sentiments on the subject of slavery. Not long after his settlement he preached this discourse, in which he demonstrated the sinfulness of slavery on moral and scriptural grounds. It was printed and widely circulated at the time, and has been reprinted again and again, both in this country and in Europe.

It presents the arguments against slavery with cumulative and exhaustive force, as they were understood by the most enlightened opponents of the system at that day; and although it contains here and there a phrase which the author, if living, would, in the clearer light of the present day, wish to change, it is scarcely less adapted to the state of public opinion now than it was in 1802. The publisher of this edition is a grandson of the author, who honors himself as well as the memory of his noble grandfather in re-issuing a discourse which received, more than half a century ago, the warm commendation of Thomas Jefferson, and of that celebrated philanthropist, Henry, Count Gregoire of France. It is refreshing to turn from the utterances of the popular divines who dishonor the name of Christianity in our day, by their defences or apologies for slavery, to the sentiments of a noble man of a preceding generation, who labored earnestly to purify the Church from the damning iniquity, and whose counsels, if they had not unfortunately been contemned, would have resulted, long since, in the freedom of every slave on the American soil.

www.ingramcontent.com/pod-product-compliance
Lightning Source LLC
Chambersburg PA
CBHW021552270326
41931CB00009B/1171